Dedicated to all the brave children who get their shots to stay healthy.

No one likes to get shots...

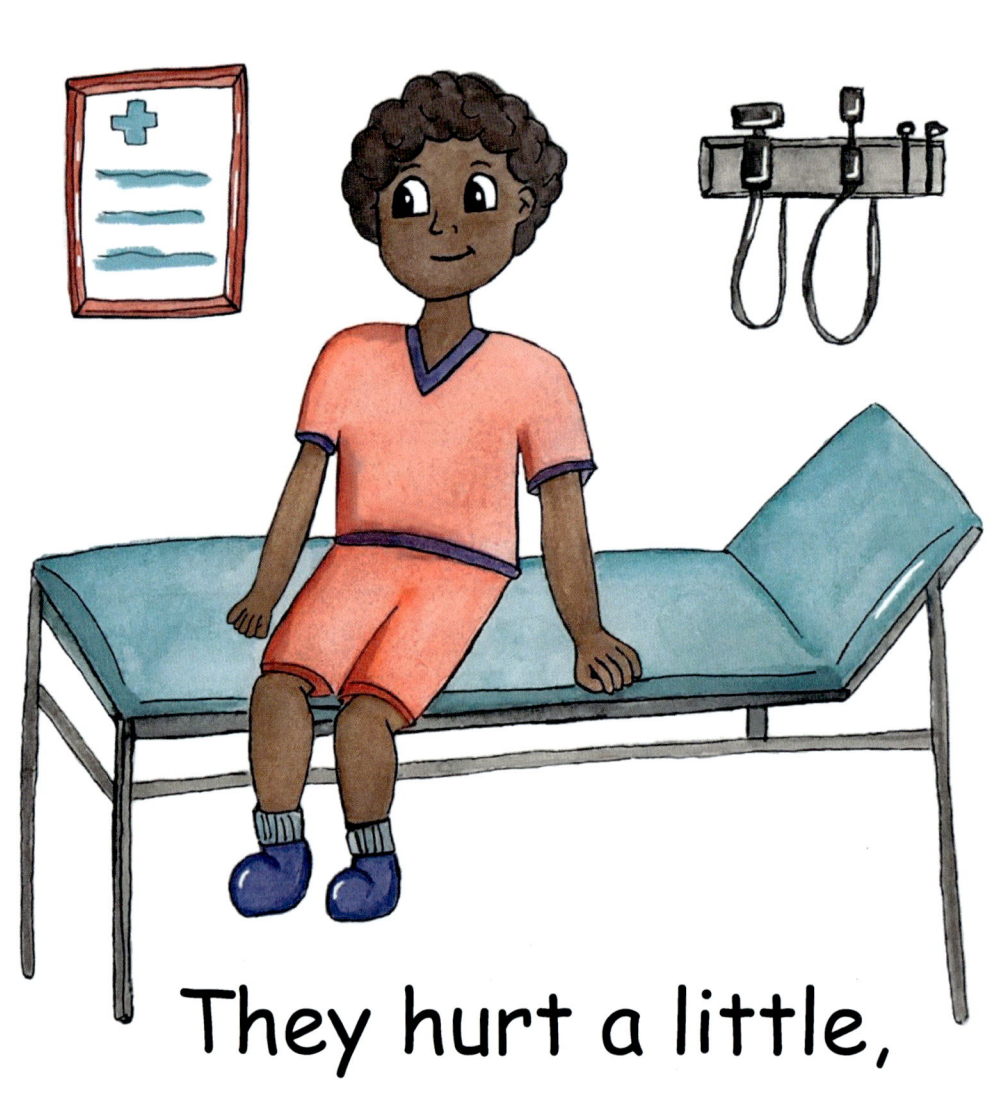

They hurt a little,

but did you know...

That shots give you SUPERPOWERS!!!

This is a story about how they work ...

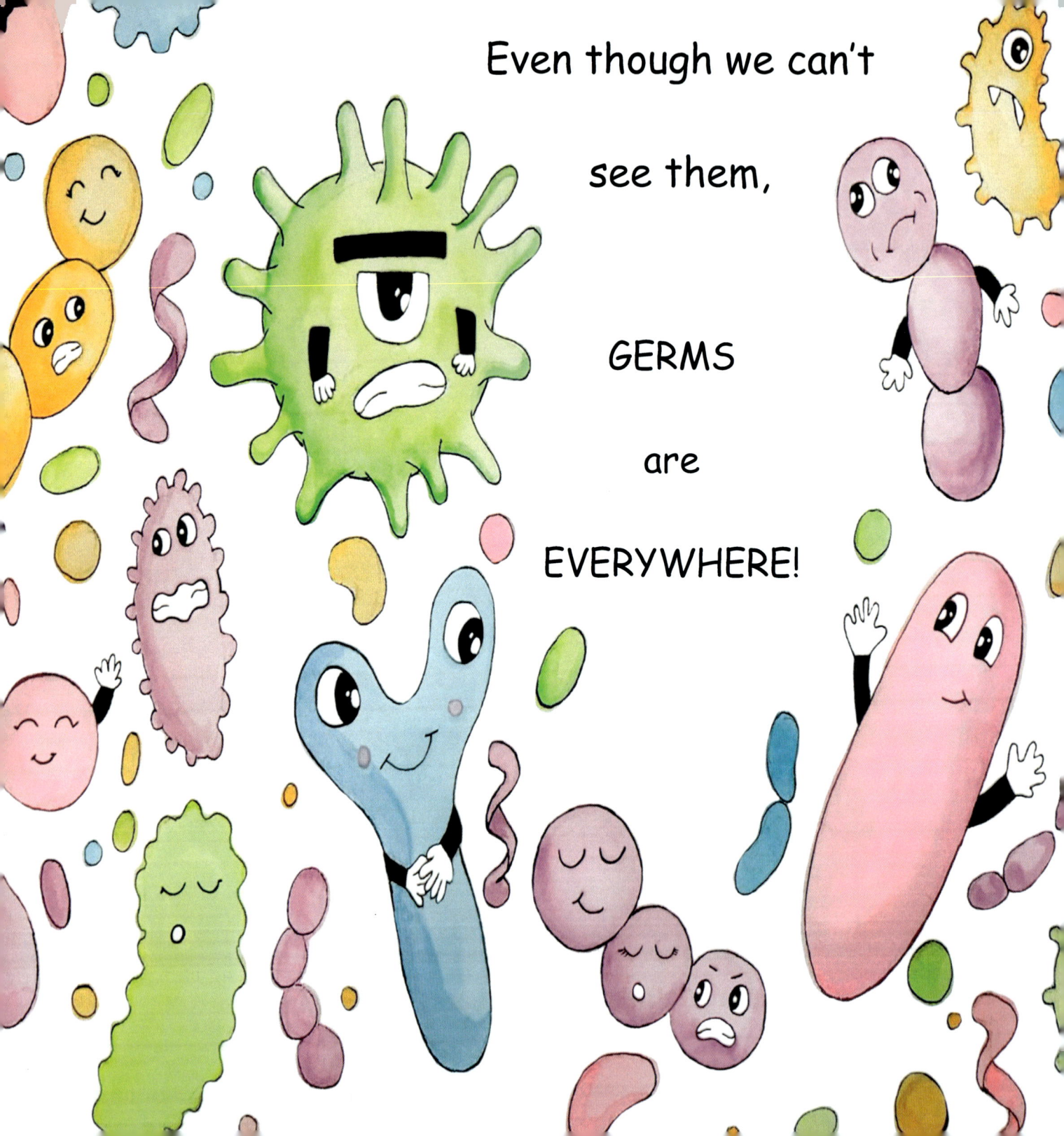

Some germs are our friends.

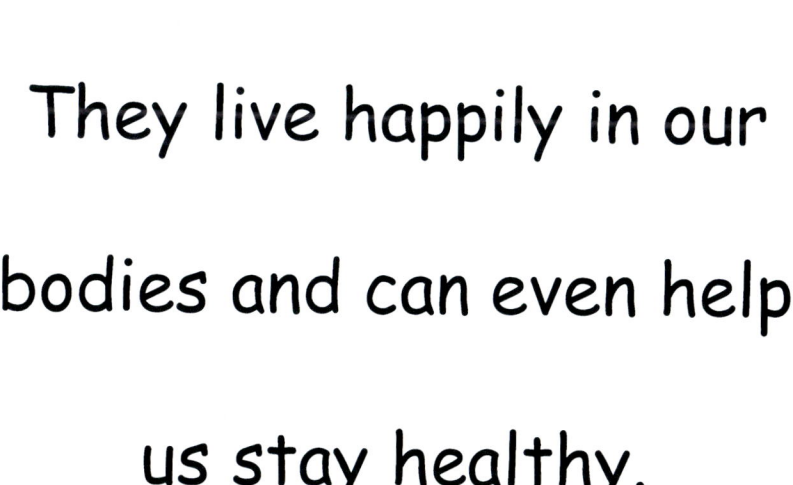

They live happily in our bodies and can even help us stay healthy.

But other germs
are not nice,
and they like to
make us sick.

Some germs can make our noses run or our heads hurt.

Others make us cough and give us belly aches!

But do not worry!

Our bodies

are amazing!

Inside our blood, we have a group of warriors ready to fight off the bad germs!

Doctors call these warriors...

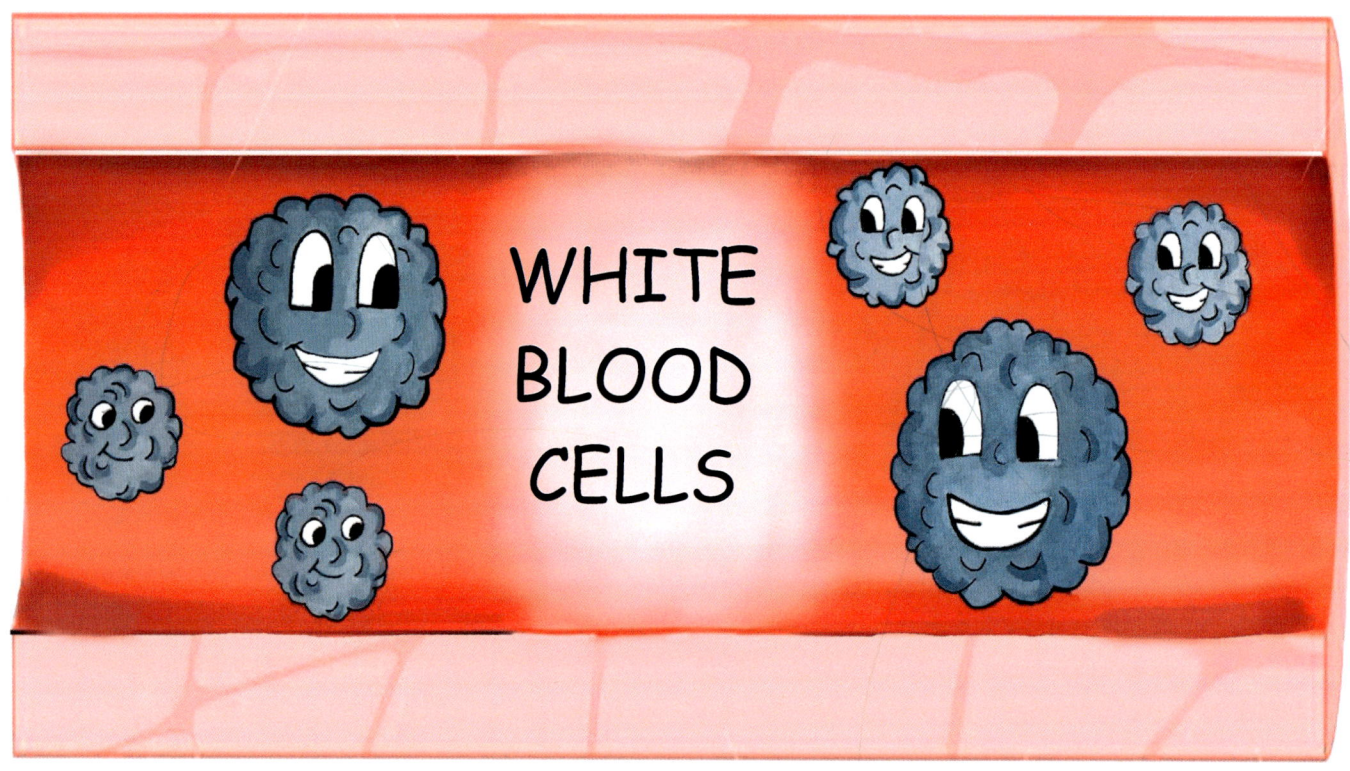

When

germs try to

make us sick,

our

WHITE BLOOD CELLS

come to the rescue and fight them off.

But sometimes, they are not strong enough on their own.

That is why shots are so important!

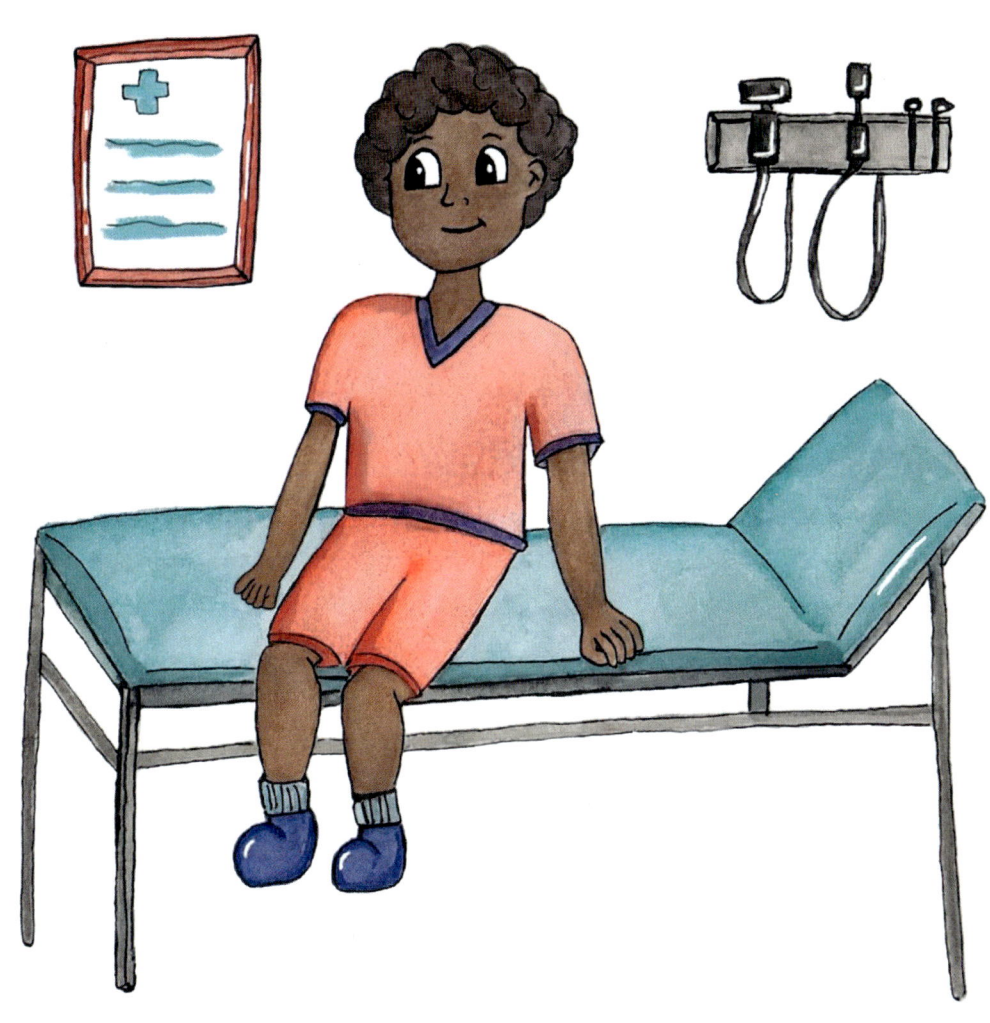

After shots, our white blood cells have swords and armour!

They have superpowers!

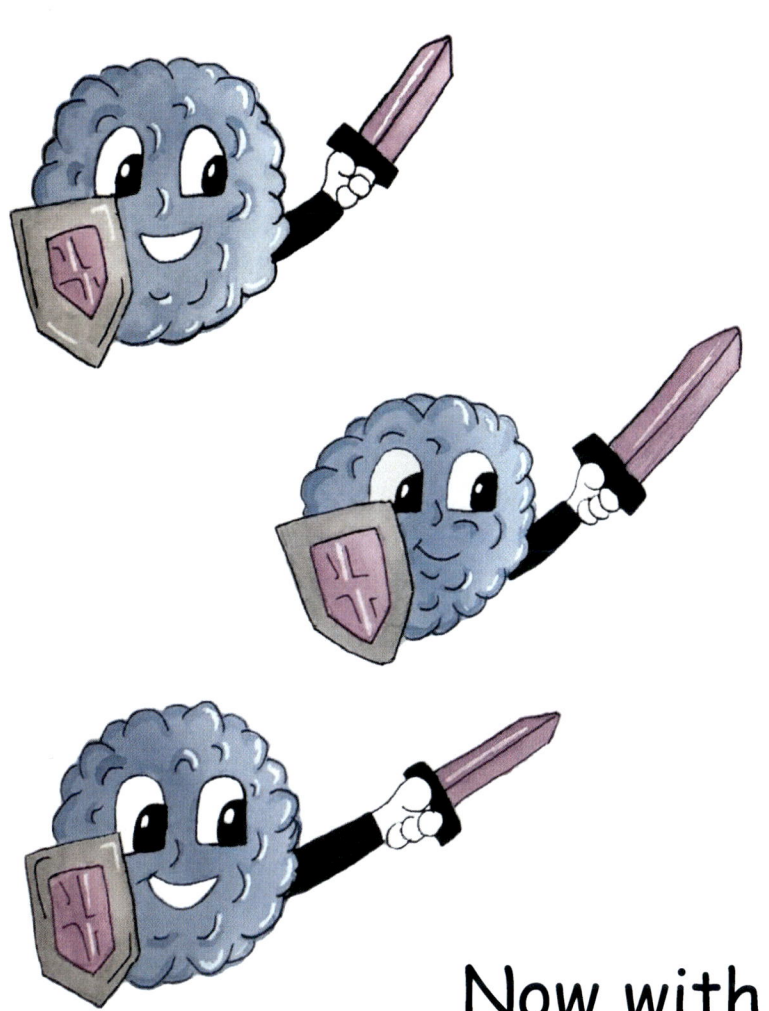

Now with their new powers they can easily fight the germs before they make you sick!

Scientists are always working hard to find new swords and armour for our white blood cells.

They even found the right swords to help beat COVID-19!

So, do not be scared of shots. They may hurt a little, but they only take a few seconds, and they give your body...

SUPER GERM FIGHTING POWERS!

Thank you for being so brave!

Made in the USA
Coppell, TX
16 September 2021